ADVANCE PRAISE FOR
NO JESUS, NO PEACE—
KNOW JESUS, KNOW PEACE

"Short, provocative, and wise, NO JESUS, NO PEACE— KNOW JESUS, KNOW PEACE is a captivating read. It reveals valuable and potentially life-changing insights to Christians and non-Christians alike."
> —CHARLES C. MANZ, author of
> *The Leadership Wisdom of Jesus* and
> *The Wisdom of Solomon at Work*

"I love the little ironic stories. . . . Each chapter [makes] a 'one-a-day' mini-meditation, something to read in the morning and think about during the day."
> —PATRICIA NAKAMURA, book and music editor,
> *The Living Church* magazine

"NO JESUS only confirms what I've taught for years: biblical principles work in every area of our lives!"
> —PASTOR MEL ROLLS, Rescue Atlanta

"Timely . . . beautifully written . . . speaks to believers and non-believers who share common enemies—self-indulgence, avarice, and a failure to be grounded in the things that truly matter."
> —T. DAVID TRIBBLE, D. Min., executive director,
> Bethesda Home for Boys

"Bless the souls of Two Seekers, who wrote with the humility of anonymity—it made this book more compelling. NO JESUS, NO PEACE is twenty-two stirring parables offering practical insights into how to live a more abundant life."
> —ALBERT GAULDEN, director, The Sedona Intensive,
> and author of *Signs and Wonders: Understanding
> the Language of God*

No Jesus,
No Peace—
Know Jesus,
Know Peace

No Jesus,
No Peace—
Know Jesus,
Know Peace

Timeless Wisdom for
Living a Life That Matters

⬛━◆━⬛

Two Seekers

WARNER BOOKS

An AOL Time Warner Company

Warner Books, Inc., 1271 Avenue of the Americas,
New York, NY 10020
Visit our Web site at www.twbookmark.com.

 An AOL Time Warner Company

Printed in the United States of America
First Printing: November 2002

10 9 8 7 6 5 4 3 2 1

Library of Congress Cataloging-in-Publication Data

No Jesus, no peace—know Jesus, know peace : timeless wisdom for living a life that
matters / two seekers.
       p. cm.
    ISBN 0-446-53076-X
    1. Christian life.

BV4501.3 .N6 2002
248.4—dc21

                                                              2002024042

Contents

Preface by Two Seekers

*Where two or more are gathered in my name,
there am I in the midst of them.*

—MATTHEW 18:19–20

W e were "the lucky ones." Soul mates born into upper-middle-class life in the early 1960s, to parents who loved each other and are, to this day, still married, we had all the trimmings of picture-perfect childhoods. Our parents respectively saw to it that we were very well educated, ensuring that we never wanted for any material thing. All in all, we had it pretty easy. But as young adults, some personal struggles surfaced.

At the age of thirty-one, one of us was diagnosed with a rare disease and eventually ended up in a wheelchair, while the other survived her own version of hell battling a variety of addictions. We both found that when you face these kinds of challenges, it serves to introduce you to yourself, and neither of us liked what we saw. To the outside world, we seemed confident and stable, but on the inside, we were both crying out to fill the God-size hole growing within each of us. Though we chose different paths, which took us years to walk, we both arrived at the same destination—finding peace in the teaching of Jesus Christ. For all of our searching and treatments, psychology and expensive specialists, we could not find lasting peace. Peace, we learned, could be found only in the solid principles by which Jesus lived.

As we began to reconnect with each other and share our faith, we felt the overwhelming, undeniable presence of Jesus between us. Excited and encouraged, we watched in awe as our faith grew and many seemingly "coincidental" occurrences began to unfold and set us on a definite path. Given that we believe in the power of the word, we felt compelled to share the peace of Jesus we had found from sharing our faith, but we also knew that we were not qualified as spiritual scholars or anyone of advanced spiritual growth. We were just two ordinary women who led unremarkable lives, yet when our souls linked together, there was a spark of divine intervention between us. It manifested itself in many different, strange, and beautiful ways. And eventually, we realized we had to share what we were learning. Fearing that egos and love of fame would defile the messages and lessons God was teaching us, we were humbled and realized that as a basic ingredient in making sure God was the source of all direction for our book, we should remain anonymous. After all, there were thousands more qualified to write a book on the principles of peace, as Jesus taught them.

And so we leave you with our simple lessons. Lessons taught to us and shown to us through countless miraculous experiences and people. As you read this little book, it is our fervent prayer that the peace of Jesus comes to you and fills your heart and soul and remains with you always.

No Jesus,
No Peace—
Know Jesus,
Know Peace

Blessed are the peacemakers,
for they shall be called the sons of God.

—MATTHEW 5:9

Introduction: Jesus Christ, Peacemaker

For unto us a child is born,
To us a son is given,
and the government will be on his shoulders.
And he will be called . . .
the Prince of Peace.

—ISAIAH 9:6

He healed the sick.
He walked on water.
He rose from the dead.

Jesus Christ, by all accounts, was both a miracle worker and a remarkable man who became one of the most towering figures of the last two thousand years. Uniting people of many lands into a great religious movement that is now the most widespread in the world, Jesus was a lightning rod for equality, justice, and the truth, as well as for the ideals of faith, hope, and love.

Absent from the public eye for most of his early life, Jesus did not emerge as a teacher in Galilee until he was thirty years old. By age thirty-three he had been convicted of high crimes, sentenced to death, and crucified in Jerusalem. What little we know of his brief public life comes from accounts in the New Testament, where Jesus is portrayed as a man of divinity who embraced society's outcasts and challenged its conventions, always using action to underscore his messages.

Welcoming prostitutes, criminals, and lepers, for instance, Jesus taught tolerance. Rejecting the stone-throwing, "eye-for-an-eye" culture of the desert world he inhabited, Jesus taught compassion. Fearlessly he presented iconoclastic advice to the large audiences he drew.

But really, when all was said and done, Jesus was a peacemaker. Offering simple, timeless lessons of acceptance and inclusion, he spoke of the need to love our neighbors with all our heart; to treat others as we ourselves want to be treated; and to turn the other cheek. Torn by war, argument, fighting, and family strife, the ancient world in which Jesus dwelled needed these messages as much as we do today.

What follows in this book is an attempt to distill the principles that Jesus taught, in his own words, and apply them to our everyday efforts to create peace in our lives. Though we may not realize it, the words we speak to one another begin ripples that spread across the globe. For better or worse, our daily words and deeds determine the climate of the world we live in. We may not be able to bring peace to the Middle East, but we can pick up the phone and smooth things over with our family members. We can be "kitchen-table" peacemakers, understanding that every little thing we do counts.

Count on Jesus for enduring principles. Keep it in mind that to know Jesus is to know peace. If you want to go for a swim in the sea of tranquillity, the Prince of Peace is waiting at the shore.

No Caring, No Peace—
Know Caring, Know Peace

————— ∞ —————

You are the light of the world.
A city on a hill cannot be hidden.
Neither do people light a lamp and put it under a bowl.
Instead, they put it on a stand,
and it gives light to everyone in the house.
In the same way,
let your light shine before men.

—MATTHEW 5:14–16

In a tale often told in Sunday school, a man once stood before God, his heart breaking from all of the pain and injustice in the world. "Dear God," he cried out, "look at all the suffering, the anguish, and the distress in Your world! Why don't You send help?" God responded, "I did send help. I sent you."

In our world today, as the saying goes, evil thrives when good people do nothing. It is not enough to just think about it; we must do something. Small actions can make a huge difference. Just as the lights from a city that sits on the hill can be seen for miles, when we show care and concern for others, an inward glow begins to surface and spread. It is impossible to hide, and it can be contagious. And yet it seems that these days, we have become masters of hiding our light.

We hide our light by being quiet when we should speak, by going along with the crowd for fear of what others will say, by denying the light within each of us, and, most of all, by not spreading the light and not caring about the needs of others.

Like Jesus, we must be beacons of caring and love, and not shut our light off from the rest of the world. All around us, every day, there are countless opportunities to show we care. Opening the door with a smile for a stranger, letting a fellow driver pull out in front of us, calling a lonely neighbor "just to chat." And in our homes we can show a sincere interest in the lives and activities of our family. Do you know your family members' favorite flavor of ice cream or the little details of their day when they are away from home? Show you care. There are a thousand different ways to do it. Start with the next person you encounter. Don't wait for the change you want to see in the world. Be the change.

FOOD FOR THOUGHT:

How can I help those around me today? Is there someone weaker than me whom I can stand up for or help in some small way? Am I going along with the crowd on an issue that I know in my heart is not right? Am I aware of some small need I could meet for those around me?

TWO

No Listening, No Peace—
Know Listening, Know Peace

Then Jesus said, "He who has ears to hear, let him listen."
—MARK 4:9

God has given us two ears and only one mouth. No doubt that's because He wants us to listen twice as much as we speak. Often we are too anxious to have our own turn at speaking and simply wait impatiently, without listening, for others to finish. There is a very big difference between really listening and waiting for our turn to talk. We fail to communicate when we do this. And we put peace at risk, because peace in our homes and in the world at large cannot be fully realized without true communication based on genuine listening.

In our family life we must learn how to "listen" not just with our ears, but also with our heart and mind. Body language, tone of voice, and demeanor are signals we send to one another, and more often than not, they are a better indicator of our true thoughts and feelings than the words themselves. Seeing the child who bows his head, never making eye contact, or hearing the soft, sad tone of a lonely person tells us more than mere words can.

As our modern world grows more complicated year by year, many of us feel overwhelmed with our lives and the demands and responsibilities of our daily routines. We long for "silent retreats" to monasteries, unspoiled nature spots, and places away from the madding crowds. This is our soul crying out for "quiet time." Time to gather our thoughts and examine what is in our hearts. Just as we often assign "time out" to our children by asking them to sit quietly in a chair and reflect on their actions, we, too, must take time out to listen to ourselves.

We must not settle for the words and babble of this world. Instead, we must cultivate silence. We must learn to cultivate the skill of listening with our hearts and minds. If we do not slow down and listen, we may miss the messages God has for us. For truly—there dwells the soul of us all.

FOOD FOR THOUGHT:

Can I go through my entire day listening to those around me, without speaking my own mind? What does this exercise in listening to others teach me?

THREE

No Kindness, No Peace—
Know Kindness, Know Peace

For out of the overflow of the heart the mouth speaks.
The good man brings good things out of the good stored up in him,
and the evil man brings evil things out of the evil stored up in him.
But I tell you that men will have to give account
on the day of judgment
for every careless word they have spoken.

—MATTHEW 12:34–36

A comedian once said that the sharpest weapon we possess is our tongue. We spend the first three years of our life learning how to use it, and the rest of our life learning how to control it.

Our home is the private space of our life that belongs uniquely to our family. There dwells a secret that seldom appears in public—our true nature. How we behave at home is often different than what we show the world. When we leave our home, we "put on" our best behavior. We speak kindly to the stranger in the elevator and to the people we work with. While we might never dream of making thoughtless, rude remarks to a waiter in a restaurant, at home we often snap at our spouse and our children, or fail to communicate at all—as if we were all roommates in some emotionless prison of our own making. Many of us are not even aware of the tone of voice we use when speaking to family members. We sometimes think that because we are in the privacy of our own home, we can indulge in a little "house-sin," taking out our frustrations and irritations on one another. Our behavior in public is like the fancy outfit we wear to church. When we return home, we take it off and hang it in the closet. But who we are at home is who we really are. Maybe the world cannot see us, but our family does. We make public declarations such as "I would die for my family!"—and yet we are not really willing to live for them.

The people in our home are God's special gift to us. That is why our goal should be to speak as kindly as possible. It is important to remember that God is the unseen guest at every meal, the unseen listener to every conversation. Our home is a sacred place; it should speak to us of reverence as clearly as our church does. In the little seeds of daily kindness grow joy and contentment. We cannot honestly lighten a family member's day without lightening our own. Our daily sentiments build the crucial peaceful home. Words can change lives. Use them thoughtfully and well.

FOOD FOR THOUGHT:

Did I speak a kind word to each member of my family today? How would my family's attitudes toward one another change if we thought of our home as a sacred place? How would we communicate with each other if we were in the presence of a church leader or someone whose morality was beyond reproach?

FOUR

No Forgiveness, No Peace—
Know Forgiveness, Know Peace

Then Peter came to Jesus and asked,
"Lord, how many times shall I forgive
my brother when he sins against me?
Up to seven times?"

Jesus answered, "I tell you, not seven times,
but seventy times seven."

—MATTHEW 18:21–22

To err is human, to forgive divine: Every schoolchild knows this adage. But human nature is also like a cooking school that teaches us to reheat our loved ones' sins for breakfast. If we forgive on Tuesday night, by Wednesday morning we are stewing up a leftover casserole of blame, resentment, and anger. We sometimes throw in a little bit of revenge as a special accent. This recipe makes for a bitter meal that can cause a lifetime of heartburn.

When we withhold forgiveness, choosing to simmer in our hurts and resentments, life becomes an endless cycle of retaliation and grudges. Repeatedly revisiting past hurts and sins serves only to harden our heart, imprisoning us in a cell of self-righteousness.

Right now, this very minute, stop the madness. Make a firm decision to find the willingness to forgive. If you can't find it in your own heart, ask for help from God—for true forgiveness comes from a place far greater than ourselves. It is not necessary to feel we are ready or able to forgive. Keeping our heart and mind open to the possibility of forgiveness allows it to find a way into our soul. It is when we steel our nerves and hang on to our anger that the passageways are blocked and forgiveness becomes impossible.

One of the ironies of forgiveness is that our adversaries may not want our forgiveness and may not be willing to say, "I'm sorry." That's okay. Forgiveness is a matter of the heart—your heart. To forgive is to set the prisoner free and then realize that the prisoner was your self.

Here's an important point to remember: Although we cannot control the hurtful acts of another, we can control our responses to them. Instead of being bitter, we can be generous. Consider why the one who hurt us was unkind. Is he hurting, too? Turn the situation around and give this person understanding instead of condemnation. Changing perspective often opens our heart.

Only through forgiveness do we rid ourselves of hurt and negative emotions and reclaim the peace we so need in our lives. Forgiveness offers freedom and tranquillity, without which we can never become the best version of ourselves.

FOOD FOR THOUGHT:

We only ask God to forgive another person when we ourselves haven't forgiven. As long as we recall the wound, we deceive ourselves if we think it is forgiven. True forgiveness does not even remember the injury.

FIVE

No Sharing, No Peace—
Know Sharing, Know Peace

If someone wants to sue you and take your tunic,
let him have your cloak as well.

—MATTHEW 5:40

Back in kindergarten, when the teacher served milk and cookies at recess, she always encouraged sharing. That meant making sure everybody got an equal portion. Born with a built-in "fairness meter," most five- and six-year-olds sounded the alarm when anyone tried to hoard or overindulge. Somehow, as we got older, we forgot our lessons, creating a world of "Haves" and "Have-Nots." Maybe that's why an estimated one hundred thousand American children go to bed hungry every night in a country that throws out fifty thousand pounds of food per day, according to hunger experts.

We need to create a world where everybody has a fair share of the chocolate chips! It can't be a world based on the obligation to share, but rather on the desire to give. For truly there is no delight in creating the inequity that gives rise to suffering. Nor should we think of sharing only in terms of money or things. Our time and talents minister to the soul more than any material good ever could.

Imagine what a harmonious world it would be if every single person, young and old, shared a little of what she was good at doing.

Everyone would be able to contribute, for even the poorest of the poor can share their heart and love. When we share from the heart in a generous way, we are lifted out of ourselves to a place of calmness, contentment, and peace.

Let us ask God, when we have an opportunity to share, to help us to be generous. For by not sharing, we do not neglect only the needs of others; most of all, we neglect ourselves.

Food for thought:

How often have we given our leftovers to the needy and felt proud of ourselves? Giving away the food we do not like, the clothes we do not wish to wear, and the articles too worn for our home does not show concern for the needy. Give until it hurts; share something that is difficult to part with. Sharing surplus is not true sharing.

SIX

No Love, No Peace—
Know Love, Know Peace

A new command I give you:
Love one another.
As I have loved you,
so you must love one another.

—JOHN 13:34

Working among the poor and dying in Calcutta, Mother Teresa once said that the only greater deprivation she had seen was in the West, where the "poverty of spirit" was profound. Her observation—that human beings who live only for themselves can obtain great material wealth and wind up spiritually bankrupt—is a profound truth. That's because money can't buy love, and only love makes us independently wealthy. Love transforms us into who we were meant to be—brothers and sisters in the family of humanity. We are here on earth to love and help one another. That is our highest purpose. The most infectiously joyous people are those who live to love and serve others. For we cannot hold a torch to light another's path without brightening our own.

As we walk on the path of love, let us remember the often told Sunday school story of the three visitors who came upon a family's house, prepared to grant a gift. The visitors' names were Success, Wealth, and Love. Upon arriving, they knocked on the door and were invited inside.

"Only one of us may enter," the three visitors told the family.

"Let us invite Wealth!" exclaimed the daughter of the house. "Then we shall never want for anything." Wise enough to know that Wealth did not secure happiness, the girl's father suggested that Success be their guest. But his wife wasn't sure. She believed that Love was the most powerful of the trio. After much discussion, the family ushered Love into their home—and Success and Wealth quickly followed.

"I don't understand," said the father. "I thought only one of you could come in."

"That is true," answered Love. "If you had picked Wealth or Success, then only one would come in. But you picked Love, and Success and Wealth follow me everywhere I go."

"Yes," said the mother, "for all good things follow love."

FOOD FOR THOUGHT:

Is it possible that the reason I feel so empty is because I hurry through my day in a madcap rat race thinking only of myself? How many burdens can I lighten this year? How many hearts can I cheer? How much love can I give away? Who in my life is unlovable, whom I can try to love? Our souls are crying out for communion. Will I answer the call?

SEVEN

No Hope, No Peace—
Know Hope, Know Peace

Jesus stopped and ordered the man to be brought to him.
When he came near, Jesus asked the blind man,
"What do you want me to do for you?"
"Lord, I want to see," he replied.
Jesus said to him, "Receive your sight . . ."

—LUKE 18:40–42

Humans can live without food for forty days, without water for about three days, and without air for about eight minutes. But we cannot survive at all without hope.

Hope is an extraordinary grace that is written on the brow of each of us. Arousing a passion for the possible, hope looks for the good in all people, regards problems as opportunities, and pushes ahead when it would be easier to quit. Hope lights a candle instead of cursing the darkness. Though we sometimes hasten our own failure by abandoning hope, hope never abandons us.

As children, most of us possessed a hardy supply of hope. When we placed our tangled ball of string into Mama's lap, we had not a care or concern that she could sort it out. We believed in magic. Life's limitations never dampened our hopes. Entering adulthood put us in touch with the "real world." Tasting fear, failure, and the monotony of daily routines taught us to put stock in "circumstances beyond our control." We stopped believing in miracles.

Now is the time to rekindle hope. Remember that no situation or circumstance is hopeless if we consider the strength of prayer and the infinite power of God. We need only place our tangled ball of troubles in His lap. Gently. With trust.

As long as we are alive, hope is there, waiting for us to partake in its wonders. Keep hope alive!

FOOD FOR THOUGHT:

In what areas of my life have I given up hope? What can I do to keep hope alive in my daily life? Is there someone around me who could serve as inspiration?

EIGHT

No Generosity, No Peace—
Know Generosity, Know Peace

Jesus sat down opposite the place where the offerings were put . . .
A poor widow came and put in
two very small copper coins worth only a fraction of a penny.
Calling his disciples to him, Jesus said,
"I tell you the truth, this poor widow
has put more into the treasury than all the others.
They all gave out of their wealth;
but she gave out of her poverty."

—MARK 12:41–44

Sunday school teachers love to tell of the proud young man who boasted to all that he had the most beautiful heart in the village. A large crowd gathered and admired his heart. It was indeed perfect, for there was not a mark or scar on it.

Suddenly a wise old man appeared, displaying a heart badly scarred with deep gouges. Set into the holes were ill-fitting pieces that created quite a hodgepodge. "Yours is the heart that looks perfect," the old man said to the proud young man, "but I would never trade with you. For you see, every scar on my heart represents a person to whom I have given my love, while the ragged pieces are gifts given in return."

The young man was stunned. He reached into his heart, tore out a piece, and with trembling hands offered it to the old man, who responded in kind. The young man now looked at his heart, bearing some jagged edges but more beautiful than ever, since the love from the old man's heart now flowed into his.

"Now you know," said the old man. "A generous heart is always best."

As we go about our busy lives, we must remember the tale of the generous heart, sometimes scarred by its habits of giving but always overflowing with peace and love.

FOOD FOR THOUGHT:

Forget the material world for a moment.

In what ways can I be generous with my heart, time, or talents?

Who in my world could use a little generosity right now?

Do I make it a practice to leave room in my heart for love?

NINE

No Tenderness, No Peace—Know Tenderness, Know Peace

People were also bringing babies to Jesus to have him touch them. When the disciples saw this, they rebuked them. But Jesus called the children to him and said, "Let the little children come to me, and do not hinder them, for the kingdom of God belongs to such as these. I tell you the truth, anyone who will not receive the kingdom of God like a little child will never enter it."

~ LUKE 18:15–17

In the dimly lit nursery a mother hums softly to her newborn as she powders his bottom with gentle caresses. She reaches for the tiny brush and combs his soft, downy hair. Carefully she lifts him up and cradles him in her arms, speaking to him in low, soothing whispers. Tracing the unique features of his tiny face with a delicate finger, she cuddles him in blankets and rocks him tenderly, his every need anticipated. He is safe and at peace in her loving arms.

Now let's fast-forward. The newborn is now a teenager:

"Get up and turn off that blasted TV!" Mother yells. "Can't anybody help me around here?" Mother is in a hurry and angry. She pushes her son's feet off the coffee table with such force she surprises even herself. "Sorry, Mom, I was gonna help you, I just got sidetracked," her son replies.

"You're always sidetracked! You are lazy and selfish, and if you think you're going out tonight, you've got another think coming!" she yells as she slams the door behind her.

How did we get from there to here? Where did the tenderness go? Although no longer innocent babies, we are all spiritual beings worthy of tender loving care. Though the chubby cheeks and the sweet cooing of infancy have faded, that is no justification for chiding, scolding, and mistreating others. Jesus said he did not give as the world gives. Do not respond in kind. Practice a new soft demeanor on yourself and let it go forth to a world longing for a mother's tender touch. As often as possible, swaddle the world in a blanket of tenderness!

FOOD FOR THOUGHT:

Must the sweetest milk of human kindness be limited to newborns? Can I learn to say strong things gently and gentle things strongly? Can I speak the truth in love, and love the truth in each?

No Prayer, No Peace—
Know Prayer, Know Peace

When you pray, go into your room,
close the door and pray to your
Father who is unseen. . . .
For your Father knows
what you need before you ask him.

—M A T T H E W 6:6, 8

While giving a tour of heaven, Saint Peter led a group of specta-
tors down a long aisle where hundreds of angels sat idle. "Why
aren't they busy?" asked one of the tourists, referring to the celestial
beings.

"Oh," Saint Peter replied, "those are guardian angels waiting to
help humankind. They leave as soon as they are summoned."

"How do I put in a request?" asked the man excitedly.

"Do you know how to pray?" answered Saint Peter.

For all that is said and written about prayer, it is really a simple
activity. In order to pray, there is no technique or protocol to learn. We
don't have to be free from sin or blameless. Nor do we have to get down
on our knees or attend a special service in a special building. Our own
little room will do. We can choose any words we would like, because we
were created to speak directly to our Creator, to sit at His table and par-

take of all the good things He has waiting for us. We don't have to change a single thing about ourselves.

As those who have tried it know, prayer changes lives. It is a universal way for our souls to communicate with a higher power, to call upon God to send His angels to assist us. We can pray to receive. We can pray for answers and guidance. There is no matter too small for prayer. Prayer is our own private conversation with God.

Prayer is a kind of calling home every day. It can bring to us a sense of serenity and at-homeness in God's universe. It can bring us renewed strength and courage. It offers a peace that the world can neither give nor take away.

Prayer is an unopened gift. Open yours and see what miracles God has in store for you.

FOOD FOR THOUGHT:

Take a moment right now and have a conversation with God. He is always there, 24/7, ready and waiting to listen to whatever we have to say.

ELEVEN

No Compromise, No Peace—Know Compromise, Know Peace

If someone forces you to go one mile,
go with him two miles.

—MATTHEW 5:41

After their father died, two brothers were arguing over the operation of his business empire. Unable to agree on anything, they hired an arbitor who made the following proposal—one brother would divide the company holdings in half and the other would get to pick which part he wanted.

Compromise is the art of meeting in the middle. It asks that we stop seeing the world in terms of black and white, of winners and losers, and allow everyone to partake of the victory. Compromise avoids the "scorched earth" mentality that takes no prisoners while embracing the concept of "win–win."

Today, right this minute, make yourself a promise. If you get into a dispute, disagreement, conflict, or argument, don't cling to your own position with knee-jerk tenacity. Don't grind down your opponent or become addicted to being right. Try seeing the situation from the other side of the table. Seek a balance among justice, fairness, and a desire to keep the peace.

When being asked to meet someone in the middle, go all the way toward a meaningful compromise. And watch miracles unfold.

FOOD FOR THOUGHT:

Am I willing to break my old familiar patterns of behavior to see what unsuspecting gifts compromise might bring to my life?

No Charity, No Peace—
Know Charity, Know Peace

So when you give to the needy,
do not announce it with trumpets,
as the hypocrites do in the synagogues
and on the streets, to be honored by men.
I tell you the truth,
they have received their reward in full.
But when you give to the needy,
do not let your left hand know
what your right hand is doing,
so that your giving may be in secret.
Then your Father,
who sees what is done in secret,
will reward you.

—MATTHEW 6:2–4

Charity begins at home—or so the saying goes. We see it embroidered on needlepoint samplers and pincushions and lap pillows at tag sales. Grandmothers seem especially fond of quoting this adage in the messages they inscribe for posterity.

But does charity begin in our homes? Are we as generous and giving to the person sitting at our own kitchen table as we are to the hungry child overseas who is pictured on the donation card we receive periodically in the mail? Do we give short shrift to our family because we "gave at the office"? Do people say about us, "She is nicer to strangers than she is to family"?

Charity is not simply the act of writing a check to an anonymous victim. It is an everyday concern. Moving through our life at breakneck speed, we sometimes forget not to be stingy with our family members, who often get just a few crumbs left over from the feast. If charity is to radiate out into the larger world, we must practice it on a small scale at home, in our daily life.

Let us also remember, as Jesus said, that charity is quiet and self-contained. Those who give alms and make a big show of it have not practiced charity. They are but gonging cymbals, full of pride and ostentation. The reward of charity is to have done it well. Charity is also blind to the cause of suffering, never discriminating against the self-inflicted wounds of those who "brought it on themselves."

As the saying goes: *Did universal charity prevail, earth would be a heaven, and hell a fable.*

FOOD FOR THOUGHT:

Wouldn't the world be a better place if nobody cared who got credit? Offenses against charity are among the most serious regrets people can have on their deathbeds. Am I living my life in such a manner as to have no regrets at the end?

THIRTEEN

No Compassion, No Peace—
Know Compassion, Know Peace

"For I was hungry and you gave me something to eat,
I was thirsty and you gave me something to drink,
I was a stranger, and you invited me in.
I needed clothes and you clothed me.
I was sick and you looked after me.
I was in prison and you came to visit me."
Then the righteous will answer him, "Lord, when did we see
you hungry and feed you, or thirsty and give you something to
drink? When did we see you a stranger, and invite you in, or
needing clothes and clothed you? When did we see you sick or in
prison and go to visit you?" The King will reply,
"I tell you the truth,
whatever you did for one of the least
of these brothers of mine,
you did for me."

—MATTHEW 25:35–39

In his book *The Moral Compass*, William Bennett shares a story written nearly a century ago by Mrs. Charles A. Lane. It tells of a small lame boy who lived with his mother, a washerwoman, in a tiny room on the second story of an old building. Each day she left her son in his wheelchair beside the window to watch the goings-on below. His sad expression only changed upon the sight of his mother returning home. Then he would smile and wave his hand gleefully, for he loved her very much.

"I wish I could help you, Mother," he said one night. "You work so hard, and I can't do anything for you."

"Oh, but you do!" she cried quickly. "It helps me to see your face smiling down at me from the window. It helps me when you wave your hand. It makes my work lighter all day to think you will be there waving to me when I go home."

"Then I'll wave harder!" said the boy.

The next evening a tired workman happened to look up and see the lame little boy smiling and waving to his mother. The man chuckled and waved to the boy, feeling better as he continued his walk home. As the days passed, more friends waved greetings to the boy. Life didn't seem quite so hard to the people in the street as they thought how difficult it must be for him.

"Tell the lad we couldn't get on without him!" one of the workers told the mother one night. "'Tis a great thing to have a brave heart. It makes us all brave, too. Tell him that."

And so she did.

While we may not be able to heal all who suffer, we must not discount the value that our soothing words or a simple wave can have on an aching heart. Many times the only thing our friends or family need, when they are faced with a challenging or painful episode in their lives, is our compassionate understanding, our careful listening, our empathetic words. They know we can't solve their problem, or make the hurt go away, but our attention, our caring, our listening and understanding can validate their pain.

Compassion is not the ability to alleviate the suffering of others. It is but the desire to do so. Resist the temptation to brush off another's problems as "trite," and refrain from judging. Even a child abuser can be viewed with compassion when we stop to consider the atrocities that person may have suffered in his own childhood.

Today, try to move past the numbness and bewilderment of the miseries of this world. Realize that there can never be total peace and joy for us until there is also peace and joy for those around us.

FOOD FOR THOUGHT:

Who in my life can teach me something if I "put myself in her skin" for a day? What frustrations and obstacles does she face? How does she view life?

FOURTEEN

No Reconciliation, No Peace—
Know Reconciliation, Know Peace

Therefore, if you are offering your gift at the altar,
and then remember that your brother has something
against you, leave your gift there in front of the altar.
First go and be reconciled to your brother;
then come and offer your gift.

—MATTHEW 5:23–24

A bone, once broken and mended, is said to be stronger in the spot that has reknit. Through nature's healing grace the break is infused with a life more vital than it had before. The same is true with a broken relationship. Through reconciliation, it becomes stronger than before, thriving on a more resilient bond that can last a lifetime.

To reconcile means to "make whole again." That sounds easy enough. But real life has a way of kicking up complications. A competitor steals a customer by unethical means—and we seethe with anger over the injustice. A vengeful ex-spouse brings us to court in a frivolous lawsuit—and we lose valuable time setting the record straight. A trusted friend talks behind our back, and we get twisted in knots over a betrayal that creates a cold war of hard hearts.

To reknit the broken bones of a relationship, we must respond to the call that comes from deep within ourselves. That may mean turning down the volume on the voice inside our head that says, *I'm not making the first move; I'm right and she's wrong.* It may mean listening to the voice that says, *Give it another try.* You care about one another and there is too much at stake to give in to bitterness. You can go to your grave being right. And what will you have gained? You will be a dead person—who was "right."

Today, try to find the healing salve of reconciliation that can make a "broken" situation whole. Pick up the phone. Write a letter. Send an e-mail. Make an attempt to reconnect. Reaching out to those who may have hurt us—or may be hurting—is the first baby step in the dynamic process of reconciliation.

Reconciliation is made mighty through God's healing powers. Through reconciliation, let us all become strong in the broken places.

FOOD FOR THOUGHT:

Have I been using my hurts as an excuse to keep my heart closed to others? What action can I take today to reach out an understanding hand to my loved one and see past my own anger into a wounded heart?

FIFTEEN

No Fairness, No Peace—
Know Fairness, Know Peace

Give, and it will be given to you.
A good measure, pressed down,
shaken together and running over
will be poured into your lap.
For the measure you use, it will be measured to you.

—LUKE 6:38

An educator being honored as "First-Grade Teacher of the Year" was asked to reveal the secret of her success. "On the first day of school I always tell my children that life isn't fair," the teacher said humbly, "but that doesn't mean we shouldn't be."

Life isn't fair. How many times have we heard those words as we have walked the path of life? Our sister was born with more musical talent and our brother came into the world a better athlete. Our best friend eats everything in sight and is naturally thin while our cousin won the lottery on the purchase of his very first ticket. The coach doesn't pick us for the team even though we play better and harder. And the stranger next door, who lives out of a trust fund, just inherited a fortune from a mysterious stranger.

For all these seeming inequities, the explanation that comes back is always the same—life isn't fair.

Let's face the facts—we have a distinct choice to make in life. We can be angry at the basic unfairness of events. We can scoff at the roll of the dice, play victim, and remind everyone we come in contact with that we got the short end of the stick. Or we can watch and learn from our teacher of the year.

"Anytime there's a birthday, I buy a big delicious cake that the celebrant must cut into a number of slices equal to the members of the class," the teacher said. "We set all the slices out and the birthday person gets the piece remaining after everyone else has selected. Fairness depends on the person who cuts the cake."

Let's not complain about the world's lack of fairness. Let's be fair and create peace and harmony each time we cut the cake. For as Jesus said, "The measure you use, it will be measured to you."

FOOD FOR THOUGHT:

Am I giving to my brother as I would want him to give to me? Can I practice fairness with my children and send them into the world with a sense of rightness and integrity?

SIXTEEN

No Communication, No Peace—
Know Communication, Know Peace

Jesus knew their thoughts and said to them, "Every kingdom divided against itself will be ruined, and every city or household divided against itself will not stand."

—MATTHEW 12:25

"We're all connected!" boasts one of the world's largest telecommunications companies. And it's true. We are all connected —by wires! Equipped with personal computers, cell phones, and fax machines, the average American home is now linked to the vast new frontier of cyberspace. People today possess the capacity to talk to any corner of the world at any time, and they can connect in a matter of seconds.

But with all the technological wizardry, has our communication become more meaningful? While chatting on the Internet with a total stranger, we ignore those who live under our own roof. The dying institution of the family dinner may soon be interrupted by an explosion of videophones. Living in this age of anonymity, we know more about the lives of Hollywood stars than we do our own extended family members. Where has all of this communication gotten us?

Let us make a frank observation: Electronic communication will never take the place of face-to-face rapport. You can't "know" someone without hearing the inflection of her voice and the look in her eye, the most essential elements of intimacy.

True communication is rooted in a magnetic and creative force called listening. The ones who listen to us are the ones we move toward. When we are listened to, it creates us, makes us unfold. Listening becomes holy when we witness someone's tale of woe without responding with one of our own.

It has been said that sainthood occurs when we give up or set aside our own prejudices, frames of reference, and desires, so as to experience the speaker's world from the inside, to step into his shoes. This unification of speaker and listener is actually an extension and enlargement of ourselves. When it occurs, we begin to appreciate one another more, and the dance of love and understanding is begun.

FOOD FOR THOUGHT:

What would I learn about my family members if I turned off the computer, fax, cell phone, and TV for an entire evening? Have I ever really truly communicated with my next-door neighbors?

SEVENTEEN

No Faith, No Peace—
Know Faith, Know Peace

A woman who had been subject to bleeding for twelve years
came up behind Jesus and touched the edge of his cloak. She said
to herself, "If I only touch his cloak, I will be healed."
Jesus turned and saw her. "Take heart daughter," he said,
"your faith has healed you."
And the woman was healed from that moment.

—MATTHEW 9:20–22

Pulitzer Prize–winning author Laura E. Richards, daughter of Julia Ward Howe, often wrote stories exploring man's capacity for tenderness toward those around him. One such story, "The Hill," tells of a small boy, discouraged and doubtful that he could ever make it to the top of a large hill. His older and wiser sister tricks him into playing a game in which the two match footprints to see whose is the best. After a while the boy looks up in disbelief.

"Why," he said, "we are at the top of the hill!"

"Dear me!" said his sister. "So we are!"

Confronted by life's problems, it often seems easier to despair. Instead of putting one foot in front of the other, confident we can make the climb, we remain stuck at the bottom. Faith is not complacent; faith is a potent mixture of belief and action. It is the big sister advising us to move our feet. When the darkness of despair descends over you, turn to the night-light of faith in possibilities greater than yourself. God has given us this gift to help us on our path to the top of the hill.

FOOD FOR THOUGHT:

Every tomorrow has two handles. I can take hold of it by the handle of worry, or the handle of faith. Which will I choose?

EIGHTEEN

No Spirituality, No Peace—
Know Spirituality, Know Peace

He who hears my words and puts them into practice
is like a man building a house, who dug down deep
and laid the foundation on rock.
When a flood came, the torrent struck that house
but could not shake it,
because it was well built.

—LUKE 6:47–48

Building sand castles is a favorite pastime for many children. As summer stretches away endlessly on hot afternoons, our little ones fill their buckets with wet sand, letting their imaginations take shape on the edge of the shore. Patting with shovels, packing with sticks, they leave their creations to bake in the sun's scorching rays. Soon night falls and the tide rolls in, devastating the most elaborate structures.

A life without spirituality is like a sand castle, buffeted by unpredictable tides and quickly brought down by powerful currents. Without the divine foundations of faith, prayer, and belief, our lives are vulnerable to the roiling waters of misfortune. If fear strikes, we find no shelter in a conversation with God. If tragedy occurs, we miss the calm harbor of faith where the hand of God may keep us from crashing against the rocks. And if injustice befalls us, we may deny what can make us whole—the power of God to bestow healing.

The castles of summer exist for a moment in time. Spirituality is eternal. Will we build like children on the edge of the water, where the deceptively gentle sea foam licks our fortress, ready to attack in the dark of night? Or will we emulate those who know that true inner peace comes by anchoring ourselves in steadfast spiritual values?

The sun is high, but night will soon fall, ushering in the tide. The choice is ours.

FOOD FOR THOUGHT:

God accepts me just as I am, right at this very moment. He is waiting for me to talk to Him, from the heart, in my own words. Will I let Him be my spiritual foundation?

Nineteen

No Humility, No Peace—
Know Humility, Know Peace

For everyone who exalts himself will be humbled,
and he who humbles himself will be exalted.

—Luke 14:11

A six-year-old boy lay in a golden field of wheat on a late summer evening with his father stretched out beside him. Gazing up at the night sky, he observed the heavenly bodies sparkling overhead. "Dad, what's out past the moon?" the boy asked inquisitively.

"The other planets, son," the father replied.

"And what's past that, Dad?" The son beamed with curiosity.

"Our galaxy, the Milky Way."

"And past that?"

"Andromeda."

"And past that?" the boy asked enthusiastically. The father chuckled at the boy's insatiable hunger for knowledge.

"Past that, there are a hundred million other galaxies, each containing a hundred billion suns, all of which they say are even bigger than our own sun."

"Wow!" the boy exclaimed, scratching his head. "But if the universe is so big and we are so small, what does God need us for?"

The father fell silent for a moment. "Well, son," he continued, "God needs me so I can take care of you." He reached over and kissed his son on the head.

It is said that the first test of a great person is humility. But humility is a paradox. For no person is humble who thinks he is. Neither does self-importance make one person better than the next. True humility is a matter of seeing in proportion. Knowing we are an infinitesimal dot in God's universe should not diminish or negate the valuable work we do in our small corner of His world. Each person is someone of consequence in God's eyes, no more or less so than any other.

Tonight, when you look out your window at God's magnificent night sky, looking for the heavenly lights, ask God to help you see in holy proportion. Humble yourself before all things and thank heaven for the inestimable role you play in the divine scheme!

FOOD FOR THOUGHT:

Humility comes long before success, not only in the dictionary, but also in the book of life. Life's path becomes easier and smoother with humility paving our way.

Twenty

No Sympathy, No Peace— Know Sympathy, Know Peace

Blessed are those who mourn, for they will be comforted.
—MATTHEW 5:4

Abeloved nurse at a busy metropolitan hospital was once asked to identify the most important ingredient in her work. "So many thoughts come to mind," she said thoughtfully, "but if I had to choose one quality above the rest, I suppose it would be sympathy, which is not to be confused with pity. While pity grows from feeling sorry for the patient, 'sympathy,' as a wise man once said, 'is about two hearts tugging at one load.'"

Life is full of situations that call for sympathy. A friend gets sick. A family gathers to grieve the loss of a loved one. A child comes home from school with a poor result on an important test. All need help to face their burden. To act in sympathy—as two hearts tugging at one load—means resisting the temptation to reinforce the "poor me" of the victim. True sympathy does not condescend to the one who suffers. It is about standing shoulder to shoulder and pulling in unison.

Today, if you see someone in need of special caring or sympathy, consider how you would want to be treated under the same circumstances. If you were sick or grieving, would you prefer a worried look of helplessness or an even-tempered display of concern? Surely those in need of sympathy are better served by a soothing voice than an avalanche of our tears.

When the voice of sympathy speaks, it says, *I am here for you, and with you.* Many times that is all a person requires to know she is not alone in her struggle. Sympathy can be the bridge that brings her from despair to hope.

We cannot truly tread another's path, but we can hold the light at his feet, steady and sure so that he may see.

FOOD FOR THOUGHT:

Where can I set aside time from my busy life and assist another who needs a helping hand of understanding? Can I set down my load for a while and help my loved ones carry theirs?

TWENTY-ONE

No Justice, No Peace—
Know Justice, Know Peace

But I tell you: Love your enemies and pray for those who persecute you, that you may be sons of your Father in heaven. He causes his sun to rise on the evil and the good, and sends rain on the righteous and the unrighteous. If you love those who love you, what reward will you get . . . And if you greet only your brothers, what are you doing more than others?

—MATTHEW 5:44–47

A group of sixth-graders touring the Federal Court Building in Washington, D.C., found themselves drawn to a statue of a robed woman holding the scales of justice in her hands. When one of the students asked the tour guide to explain why the lady was wearing a blindfold, he said, "To prevent her from being distracted from the truth."

When seeking justice to rectify the upsets of our everyday life, it's so easy to be distracted by what doesn't apply. Our brother "borrows" our favorite shirt without asking—and we dredge up every wrong he ever committed over our lifetimes together. Our children "explain" what happened to the homework they didn't turn in—and we fret about their chances for getting into college. A friend doesn't deliver the apple brown Betty she "promised" to fix for the bake sale we are chairing—and we decide we need an apology written in blood and nailed to the front door of the cathedral.

Here are a few home truths about justice that may be worth bearing in mind.

First, justice does not get distracted by feelings and passions. It is divorced from vengeance and is blind to revenge.

Second, justice allows for a peaceful outcome by safeguarding a well-balanced sense of proportion. To achieve justice, we must steel ourselves against the temptation to "win" our case by exaggerating the facts on which our case rests.

Finally, justice looks forward, never back. Not intent on rectifying every past infraction ever committed since the dawn of time, justice remembers that it is a sister to forgiveness. Restoring an even walkway is needed so that all parties involved can go forward.

If you are struggling with a family dispute, an argument, or a rift that seems beyond repair, pray for justice. Pray for the objectivity and enlightenment to cradle it in your heart, never meeting an evil with an evil, but only valuing the good. Don't be blind to what is right. Seek peace by being open to justice for all involved.

FOOD FOR THOUGHT:

Who in my life have I judged unfairly? Can I see him differently by striving to be like Lady Justice—blindfolded to the distractions?

TWENTY-TWO

No Humanity, No Peace— Know Humanity, Know Peace

For whoever does the will
of my Father in heaven
is my brother and sister and mother.

—MATTHEW 12:50

A philosopher once said that whichever way we see the world, we will be exactly right. If we see dishonesty in our life, we will be surrounded by dishonest people. If we see giving hearts, we will be surrounded by good and decent people. What we see is what we get.

As we go forward in life, let it be our goal to find the good in humanity, and praise it. Let's look for kindness, caring, mercy, goodness, tenderness, and compassion in our fellows. Let's single these out and sing their virtues. Let's reinforce the very best in humanity and encourage it to grow like a seed in the sunshine. Envisioning ourselves as branches on the tree of life, together bearing fruit and filtering the light, let's cultivate the best in ourselves and others so that the new growth is healthy and strong.

Let us look to Jesus Christ, the condescension of divinity and the exaltation of humanity, as the roots of our tree, anchoring us for all time in the most fertile soil.

FOOD FOR THOUGHT:

It is said that we are spiritual beings having a human experience. How can I add to the human experience in a positive way drawing from the spiritual power that is available to me?